The Best of Friends

The Best of Friends

CLASSIC

ILLUSTRATIONS

OF

CHILDREN

AND

ANIMALS

COMPILED AND EDITED BY PAMELA PRINCE

HARMONY BOOKS/NEW YORK

Copyright © 1991 by Pamela Prince

Published by Harmony Books, a division of Crown Publishers, Inc.,
201 East 50th Street, New York, New York 10022. Member of the Crown Publishing Group.

HARMONY and colophon are trademarks of Crown Publishers, Inc.

Manufactured in Hong Kong

Library of Congress Cataloging-in-Publication

Prince, Pamela.
The best of friends: classic illustrations of children and animals/edited by Pamela Prince.——1st ed.
p.   cm.
Summary: Old illustrations that depict children with animal friends are accompanied by
descriptive prose and poetry.
1. Animals——Literary collections.   [1. Animals——Literary collections.]   I. Title.
PZ5.P78685Be   1991
741.6——dc20   90-29852
                                                                                    CIP
                                                                                    AC

Design by John Fontana

ISBN 0-517-57620-1

10   9   8   7   6   5   4   3   2   1

First Edition

For Ann and Susan

INTRODUCTION

When I was a child, my family always had pets, and this set the stage for a life filled with the joys of animals; I've never been without at least one. My first pet was a big black-and-white cat named Cookie. I can remember the scent and feel of her soft fur and fondly recall holding her close to hear her purr. Spoken words had little to do with our relationship, as they have little to do with many of childhood's souvenirs. Children live in a world directed by the senses, as animals seem to do, and when the two meet, there arises an immediate bond, providing a sense of security, of pleasure, and of quiet understanding. The realm of adults, complete with words and abstractions, floats above a child's comprehension, while animals exist within the child's province.

Animals teach children friendship and loyalty, gentleness and kindness, and responsibility, too. They teach about birth and death and about the precious life to be experienced in between. My young son quickly learned that cats may scratch when their tails and ears are pulled, and that tender persuasion can be far more effective than force——a useful lesson to learn at any age. When we had to bury a fragile, still bird in the garden, I'm certain he felt a new awareness of his own breath and being. Also, animals are fun. One night when I was about three, I watched my pet cat give birth to a litter of lively kittens. A miracle, it seemed! The spheres of tumbling fur fascinated me and my brothers, and, although I can't count the numbers of kittens and puppies I've been around since, each one seems a delightful mystery. Young animals, human and otherwise,

share a kind of boundless and diffuse energy, scattered about with frisky and abundant exuberance. The only creature more indefatigable than a four-year-old boy is his puppy.

For the images included in this book, I am grateful to those artists who found something sweet and touching, funny or sad, sensitive and lovely, in their subjects. Some are unabashedly sentimental, some humorous, some delicately profound. All capture some aspect of that emotional range, exchanged between innocents, where understanding is reached without speech, where trust is implicit, and where love runs deep.

Advertisement for Pears Soap. c. 1890

8

Anna and Reilly tucked Chessie into bed, gently arranging the soft sheets around the little kitten's body and fluffing the cool pillow beneath its head. As soon as Chessie looked snug and drowsy, the children said their evening prayers, adding a special thought at the end, "...and don't forget Chessie."

L. Thomas, illustrator, 1936

Ben gently held the little duckling, looking quietly into the young bird's eyes. The boy stroked the downy feathers with his small hand and the duck nestled in to his chest with a soft *peeping* sound. Neither knew how to speak, but that didn't matter; they felt happy and could trust one another implicitly.

Maud Tousey Fangel, illustrator, 1924

Albertine's a thirsty cat,
So Chris begins to pour
A little milk into her bowl.
She meows, "More, please, more."

"You know how much I love you;
You're the cat that I adore.
But don't you think you've had enough?"
She meows, "More, more, more."

"I really think," says Christopher
(I've mentioned this before),
"That you are getting very plump,"
She meows, "More, more, more."

"I'll give you just another taste,
But then I shall ignore
Requests for even one more drop..."
She meows, "More, more, more."

Jessie Willcox Smith, illustrator

I would like to give you some, Marcel, but Mama said I mustn't."

The cat seemed unable to understand Sophie and continued to stare with intent at both the girl and her drink.

"Cats don't even like tea!" said Mama softly. "But we do have a bit of fresh cream left from breakfast..."

Marcel's ears perked up. "Come with me!" Sophie said with a smile. "I shall pour your cream into a proper cup and saucer!"

Theophile Steinlen, illustrator, c. 1895

11

EASTER
NUMBER

LIFE

PRICE, 10 CENTS
VOL. LVII, NO. 1484   APRIL 6, 1911
COPYRIGHT, 1911, LIFE PUBLISHING COMPANY

A FRIEND OF THE FAMILY.

C. COLES PHILLIPS

unchtime!" Catherine announced as she distributed carrots to the five plump rabbits she had helped raise from the time they were born. The rabbits wasted no time. They twitched their ears, wriggled their noses, and got right down to the serious business of munching....

H mmm," thought Lydia, a curious little girl who *never* could seem to keep out of mischief. "I wonder what purple Easter egg dye would look like on Priscilla's clean white fur coat?"

Coles Phillips, illustrator, 1911 and 1912

13

14

ook! He's got a worm!"
cried Joan.

"No," said Uncle. "That's his tongue.
He is an anteater, and he lives
almost entirely on ants. First, with
those sharp claws he pulls down
their nests, which in South America
are often very large. Out pour the
ants to see what is the matter, and
he just flicks that saliva-covered
tongue here, there, and everywhere
until there is scarcely one left...."

So Wallie put out his tongue.
The anteater did not seem to think
much of it.

Outside the Parrot House, everybody wanted first of all to look at the long line of gorgeous, hooked-beaked creatures under the trees. They all had hooped metal perches and little trays of food, and while some looked solemn and very bored, others looked cross and extremely wide-awake. A few sat upright, as good birds should, and some hung head downward, or held on to their perches cornerwise with one claw only, as if to say,"*You couldn't do that now, could you?*"

Margaret W. Tarrant, illustrator
Harry Golding, author *Zoo Days*, 1919

I learned to spell a new word today at school," declared Christine to her favorite cat, Colette. The little girl set down her book bag and pulled out a tablet. It was difficult for her to write with the kitty attacking her pencil at every stroke, but Chris somehow managed to carefully inscribe three letters on the board: "'C' and then an 'A' and now a 'T'...there, that spells 'Cat.' Aren't you proud of me?"

GOOD HOUSEKEEPING

APRIL, 1918   15 CENTS

The goldfish swimming in their bowl set Adam's daydreams into a pleasant spin. The shimmering orange darts of color circling lazily, playing hide-and-seek in between the floating green plants, made him think of angelfish and sharks, eels and seahorses, and all the creatures he liked visiting at the aquarium. He took a pinch of food and dropped it into the water. "Here's a little snack," he called down into the bowl that held his imaginary world.

17

Jessie Willcox Smith, illustrator, c. 1930 and 1918

Allan loved the barn in the early morning, the warmth of the horses, and the smell of the hay and wood. "Hello, Porter," he called, "let's get ready for a ride." The collar was almost the worst part of the business, so heavy was it for a young man to lift....

18

Jessie Willcox Smith, illustrator

Maria lifted up a large, silky ear and teased Louis for a minute. "You'd like a bite, wouldn't you?" The patient Saint Bernard resisted eagerly lunging toward the tempting piece of bread. "Here you are," she laughed. "I'm happy to share anything with you!" He swallowed the treat and rewarded Maria's generosity with a nuzzle. In return, she lovingly pet his great, gentle head.

19

Paul Wagner, illustrator, 1907

W here did you come from, butterfly,
Floating like petals and fluttering by?
Soft as a whisper, the hum of your wings
Sings of the world's miraculous things;
I'm glad, of all places, the back of my hand
Is the place that you chose when you
     wanted to land.

20

Anonymous illustrator, c. 1885

H e saved Josephine!" cried Alex from the shore, while Camille comforted little Delia, who was fretting that she'd never see her doll again. Meanwhile, Randolph the spaniel paddled steadily toward the rocks where he gently laid down the wet and weary Josephine, who had suffered quite a fright during her unexpected ordeal at sea. "You are our hero, Randy! Hip, hip and hooray!"

Anonymous illustrator

A kangaroo carrying her baby is not seen every day. One little girl had a doll in her hands. Mrs. Kangaroo spread out her forelegs as much as to say, "See! Mine is a much better way. Why don't you carry your babies like this? No need to use your hands at all."

Margaret W. Tarrant, illustrator

Harry Golding, author *Zoo Days*, 1919

The hen trusted Evan now. He had been out every morning to say "hello" to her chicks and seemed to know how to behave gently and quietly around them. The fluffy babies nibbled the feed that the boy brought and their mother pecked a bit of it right out of Evan's steady palm. "Here you are," he murmured. "Have some breakfast."

23

Alice Beard, illustrator

"We share our fun," the puppy thought.
"We share our games and smiles.
Now, if she's sad, I'll share with her
the corner for a while."

Bessie said to Morgan,
"Let's be pals for evermore.
We'll share the good times and the bad.
That's what friends are for."

Bessie Pease Gutmann, illustrator

5294 CURLY HEAD

The baby chick, an airy bit of downy feathers, cuddled into the nest of Jeanie's hand. "Good morning," she said softly.

G̲ood news today!" sang the proud and happy mother bird. "Congratulations!"
offered Norma after seeing the bird's new family. The four tiny baby birds
cheeped in their nest and Skipper greeted them with a welcoming *woof....*

Mabel Rollins Harris, illustrator

Rough had only once been to the town before, so it was a great treat for him. I polished up the little bit of brass on his collar, and then brushed him, and made him look very smart. He followed beautifully. "Good dog!" I said to him, and he wagged his tail. . . .

Honor C. Appleton, illustrator
Mrs. H. C. Cradock, author *Josephine,
John, and the Puppy*, c. 1920

Barbara heard a clattering and chattering right outside her window, where she had left an assortment of nuts. Pulling the curtain aside, she saw three squirrels. "This is the season for us to tap the syrup out of the maple trees," she chided, "and here you are, spending your time playing and swinging in the hammock!"

29

Anonymous illustrator

30

Betty and Bob have many friends. One is their cat, Tabby, who mews and purrs.
Another is their dog, Rover. How he can bark! Dick is their canary.
He sings and sings and sings so sweetly.

Polly is their parrot. He can talk. He talks like Betty and Bob. He meows like
Tabby. He barks like Rover. And sometimes he tries to sing like Dick, the canary.
It is fun to hear him try to sing. Betty and Bob always laugh when Polly
tries to sing. Then Polly laughs, too.

Maud and Miska Petersham, illustrators
Robert Foresman, author
La Velle Bobolink Book, 1922

Oh, how I wish I had a dog
   That liked to stay at home,
Who'd live with me and play with me
   And never want to roam.

Of course, I've got this little dog
   But he can't settle down.
He just comes home to eat his meals
   And then runs back to town.

Oh yes, he is a popular dog——
   'Most anyone can see——
And he likes everybody else
   As well as he likes me.

31

Katharine Sturges Dodge, illustrator
Carrie Jacobs-Bond, author
Tales of Little Dogs, 1921

Oh! Such a sight he was, covered with horrid-smelling mud. "The only thing to do," said Cook, "was to take him to the tub under the pump in the yard and give him a good bath." She gave us a big piece of soap and a towel. So off we carried him and put him into the tub.

Pat did not like being bathed
at all. He hated the soap, which
would get into his eyes; but
afterwards he was so glad to be
clean that he frisked about and
would not let us have the towel to
dry him. We had quite a tug-of-
war, and I'm afraid the towel got
rather torn. At last we took him
to the kitchen to ask Cook to
let us dry him by the fire.

THE TUG
of WAR

33

Anne Anderson, author and illustrator
The Patsy Book

The elephant took a great deal of notice of the children and especially of Joan.
There were children all round him, and children all over him, but Joan was the one
he singled out. Was it, she wondered, that he liked her new coat? Not a bit.

She carried a paper bag filled with peanuts!

I dreamt about riding on a giraffe," said Joan proudly. "It had an *awfully* long neck and its legs were as tall as Uncle. You couldn't get onto its back without climbing up its tail. And every now and again I held out a carrot and the giraffe would bend his neck to get it, and then the children would move along up to his head."

"They'd fall off," said Phil.

"They didn't. I told them to hold tight and put their arms round each other. Only one boy fell off, but that was because he hadn't got properly on before the giraffe started to walk...."

35

Margaret W. Tarrant, illustrator

Harry Golding, author *Zoo Days*, 1919

Little maid, little maid,
  Whither goest thou?
Down in the meadow
  To feed my cow.

Bell-horses, bell-horses,
What time of day?
One o'clock, two o'clock,
Off and away.

Anonymous author and illustrator
Mother Goose, Donohue edition, 1934

At the pasture gateway now,
Moo, moo, I hear our cow;
Happy in the sun or showers,

She comes home from grass and flowers;
She brings milk for us and then
To her pasture goes again.

39

"Cluck, cluck," now says the hen.
"Cluck," she calls her chicks again.
"Cluck," she says, and "Peep," say they.

Bedtime's come for them today.
Soon the baby chicks will rest
Warm beneath their mother's breast.

Janet Laura Scott, illustrator
John G. Bowman, author
Happy All Day Through, 1917

40

You have to believe in happiness,
Or happiness never comes . . .
Oh, that's the reason a bird can sing—
On his darkest day he believes in Spring.

Anonymous illustrator
Douglas Malloch, author

$\mathcal{S}$ide by side, by the waterside,
Blackie and Abigail
sit snug in the sun; she swings her feet,
he dips his wagging tail.
Side by side, by the waterside;
The song for this afternoon
is of summer's warm weather,
just being together;
True friendship's perfect tune.

41

Piglhein, illustrator